Momentary Stay

THE DREAMSEEKER POETRY SERIES

Books in the DreamSeeker Poetry Series, intended to make available fine writing by Anabaptist-related poets, are published by Cascadia Publishing House under the DreamSeeker Books imprint and often copublished with Herald Press. Cascadia oversees content of these poetry collections in collaboration with the DreamSeeker Poetry Series Editor Jeff Gundy (Jean Janzen volumes 1-4) as well as in consultation with its Editorial Council and the authors themselves.

1 On the Cross
   By Dallas Wiebe, 2005
2 I Saw God Dancing
   By Cheryl Denise, 2005
3 Evening Chore
   By Shari Wagner, 2005
4 Where We Start
   By Debra Gingerich, 2007
5 The Coat Is Thin
   By Leonard Neufeldt
6 Miracle Temple
   By Esther Stenson
7 Storage Issues
   By Suzanne Miller
8 Face to Face
   By Julie Cadwallader-Staub
9 What's in the Blood
   By Cheryl Denise
10 The Apple Speaks
   By Becca J. R. Lachman

11 Momentary Stay
    Barbara Esch Shisler
12 What the Body Knows
    By Jean Janzen
13 Cadabra
    By Jen Kindbom

Also worth noting are two poetry collections that would likely have been included in the series had it been in existence then:

1 Empty Room with Light
   By Ann Hostetler, 2002
2 A Liturgy for Stones
   By David Wright, 2003

Momentary Stay

poems by
Barbara Esch Shisler

DreamSeeker Poetry Series, Volume 11

DreamSeeker Books
TELFORD, PENNSYLVANIA

an imprint of
Cascadia Publishing House LLC

Cascadia Publishing House orders, information, reprint permissions:
contact@CascadiaPublishingHouse.com
1-215-723-9125
126 Klingerman Road, Telford PA 18969
www.CascadiaPublishingHouse.com

Momentary Stay
Copyright © 2015 by Cascadia Publishing House LLC
All rights reserved
DreamSeeker Books is an imprint of Cascadia Publishing House LLC
Library of Congress Catalog Number: 2014043471
ISBN 13: 978-1-68027-002-0
Book design by Cascadia Publishing House
Cover photo by Marilyn Nolt and cover design by Gwen M. Stamm

The paper used in this publication is recycled and meets the minimum requirements of American National Standard for Information Sciences—Permanence of Paper for Printed Library Materials, ANSI Z39.48-1984.1984.

Unless otherwise indicated Scripture quotations are from the *Good News Bible*. Old Testament copyright ©American Bible Society 1976; New Testament copyright © American Bible Society 1966, 1971, 1976.

The poem "The Word," originally called "Path," received a 2006-07 poetry contest honorable mention *Presence: An International Journal of Spiritual Direction*

Versions of poems in this collection have appeared in various outlets. For a complete listing, see Acknowledgments section, back of book.

Library of Congress Cataloguing-in-Publication Data
Shisler, Barbara Esch.
  [Poems. Selections]
  Momentary stay / Barbara Esch Shisler.
    pages ; cm. -- (Dreamseeker poetry series ; volume 11)
    ISBN 978-1-68027-002-0 (softcover : acid-free paper)
  I. Title.
  PS3569.H5623A6 2015
  811'.54--dc23
                                    2014043471

20 19 18 17 16 15   10 9 8 7 6 5 4 3 2 1

*To Harold and our children,
Kirk, Konrad, Kari*

with

thanks to Evie and Mary Lou for help in bringing these poems together.

"The figure a poem makes . . . ends in a clarification of life—not necessarily a great clarification . . . but in a momentary stay against confusion."
—Robert Frost, from "The Figure a Poem Makes."

Contents

Part I: Love—Thou art Veiled
Being Saved   17
Black and White at the Family Reunion   18
Friended   20
A Simple Little Cookie   21
Valentine's Day   22
January Birthday   23
Why   24
Dinner   25
Picking Raspberries   26
Glad Day   27
Family Reunion Photo   28
Take Lifesavers When You Go   30
Mother's Day in the Caribbean   31

Part II: There's a certain Slant of light
A Certain Knowledge   35
Evening in the Nursing Home   36
Nancy   37
First Anniversary   42
Consider the Jaws   43
Dragon Cave   44
African Violets   45

Measuring my Life   46
Old Women   47
Stories   48

PART III: PROVOCATIONS
The Gospel of Mark   51

PART IV: I DWELL IN POSSIBILITY
All Summer Blue   61
Carolina Banks   62
Dreams   63
Insomnia   64
Heaven   65
Villanelle   66
The Word   67
Hanging On   68
Easter Visit   69
The Bowl   70
After the Evening News   71
Moving the Bees   72
The Field   73
Walk in November   74
Watching Candles on Christmas Eve   75
At Centering Prayer   76
To the Mountain   77
Longing for Freedom   78
There is a Way   79

The Author   81

Momentary Stay

I

Love—Thou art Veiled
—E. Dickinson

BEING SAVED

An old man
crouches in a November rain
calling a little dog.

From the dark cage in a puppy mill
to the universe of a fenced yard,
she runs wild, drenched and trembling,
desperate for what she doesn't know.

His sciatica aches.
He chases, pleads, swears, plots.
He stays with her through
the cold afternoon,

until help comes and she is caught,
carried, wrapped, warmed,
held fast—
home.

BLACK AND WHITE AT THE FAMILY REUNION

Virginia dusk, and we gather on the farmhouse porch,
candles, poems, and hymnbooks in hand
for familiar family rituals.
We begin with the poems, each choice
haunted by an afternoon quarrel
that tastes bitter even now after ice cream.
We cradle in our aging bones the angst
of childhood; the grandchildren watch,
the in-laws clench their teeth.

Will there ever be a morning? cries Emily;
The quality of mercy is never strained;
Something there is that doesn't love a wall.
Poem follows poem in mixed voices.
When 8-year-old Ben tunes his guitar,
we sing "Down in the Valley"
in careful time to his tender pluckings.

A white cow comes to the fence at the sound of singing.
She stares, rapt and motionless, through the hymns:
The Lord is my Shepherd;
Blest be the tie that binds.
Is she curious, amused, devout?
Who can resist the impulse of laughter?

Once when I was Ben's age,
I stood at our farmhouse window
and shouted at my family,
"I only love Blacky (a cow) and Jesus!"

Black or white,
icon or bovine,
the holy cow.

FRIENDED

"Go, sit in your cell," Abba Moses said,
"and your cell will teach you everything."
You will be saved
in solitude, silence, contemplation,
the heart to heart grapple with God,
the poverty of spirit Jesus blessed.
No matter if you are dead lonely.
Die if you must. That will be blessed too.

From my lonely cell, I key in a password.
Will you be my friend—
and suddenly, friends, and friends
of friends (of friends) pop up
until a babbling host thickens my sky
and the dazzle sends me fleeing
to the end of a long lane to a barn
where brown animals chew in silence.

A SIMPLE LITTLE COOKIE

She'd be surprised to know her small words got handed down generations, spreading out to extended family until the fact of her existence is permanently established. I just visited the site where my four grandparents and parents are buried. My sisters and brothers stood at a grave where that faraway person lay in a row with her sisters, a brother, her mother and grandmother, our great-Aunt Barbara, 100 when I last saw her. I'm 9, scared of cousin Lena's vacant eyes, thin face, wisp of hair, fluttering of fingers asking her mother for a simple little cookie. When I offered my grand-daughter snacks this afternoon she grinned, "A simple little cookie will do."

VALENTINE'S DAY

Here now,
February 14, and lovers are on a stroll.
Each step is a knife
as we move through the corridor
outside my hospital room.
You steer the narcotics pole,
I, the rich juices that drip into my
wrenched body through reamed veins.

Young lovers wine and dine tonight,
dance in candlelit splendor,
see forever in the flame of
health and beauty, laughter and youth.

My dance is a gray shuffle
of institution wear and unwashed hair
beside you, dear one, helping me on.
I hear a song about love,
A many splendored thing,
that lights up the corridors
of my healing heart.

JANUARY BIRTHDAY

70 in January,
a new decade in a new year,
a new month on a bright morning,
everything new
except the flesh,
counting pills,
the vials of memory spilling.

Old and new make love all day,
their souls curved close
against chill and darkening,
holding the sweet warm pulse
that passes between them
a knowing and a praising;
that sings in a quavering voice
some hymn about love and lasting.

WHY

Why does the great congregation
gasp in one stunned breath,
fall silent, and begin to weep?

The young mother
is speaking softly
at the funeral of her uncle,
a beloved man, so kind
he seemed too good for the world
with his Down syndrome eyes
and slow sweet speech.

The young mother
is remembering
her Uncle Allen's urgent
earnest question
as she was about to give birth:

If you have a baby like me...
will you keep him?

DINNER

I roasted the turkey. The family ate it.
Ate it some more as it stretched and shrank.
Boiled it down and scraped the grease.
A crow snatched its tailbone into the air.

And now we have come to the final soup.
Morsels of meat and excellent broth,
Thanksgiving dinner swallowed with a prayer.

We bless the egg, the fledgling and hen,
disseminating spirals warm in our flesh,
moving through us to God knows where.

PICKING RASPBERRIES

Part the furred and prickly bush
Within the garden of delight,
Find the berry red and lush
Capped neatly on its counterpart;
Pluck and leave the wee stem white,
A clapper rent, its bell once rung,
Summer kisses, then takes flight,
But memory lingers on the tongue.

GLAD DAY

Gladness comes with me
when the clock chimes ten
and I put the house to bed.
Tired spouse already down.
The dog trots sweetly to her crate
crunching a biscuit.

On the table the daffodils
so yellow they lit my eyes all day.
Books and yarn away,
the candles out.
Gladness walks with me.

I set my cup in the sink,
see the crumbs he left
making his sandwich for tomorrow.
The refrigerator hums,
cooling the leftover stew from supper.

I will hold this day for a future day
when anguish comes with me instead.

FAMILY REUNION PHOTO

Like rounding up cats—
collect a few,
and others have run off
to something quicker than
the family reunion
photograph.

We document the changes:
who has grown bigger, or shrunk
an inch or more, who is absent, and
the uneasy question, why?
Who is happier this year and
who is still grimly enduring?
We try to hold together
a coat of fraying threads.

100 years from now
my great great-grandchild
may stare at today's photo,
see my smiling face,
and ask who I am
with my arms reaching out
to enfold my family.

At home, I hung the picture
of a 100-year-old family reunion;
the littlest boy is my father-in-law,
the children in a row on the grass.
All adults are as plain and severe

as a meeting of old Mennonites,
every person now dead.
Yet they lived and reunioned
with the same hope and need I have,
lined up and faced the camera
and the future
that flicks a tail
flighty and
unconcerned.

TAKE LIFESAVERS WHEN YOU GO

He rocked her out of her coat,
his hair a shock of white
above his snowy shirt and black string tie,
her purple silk blouse a hopeful match
for the sweatpants; turquoise beads
and turquoise hairpiece paired and fixed.

They held each other's hands
as they traveled the vast lobby,
chose durable, twin gray chairs to wait.

*Take lifesavers when you go
to the hairdresser,* he said.
There's a roll in my top drawer.

From a skylight
a bridge of sunshine
crossed over their heads.

The lab will find and report
which one will be left.

MOTHER'S DAY IN THE CARIBBEAN

Bathed in amniotic waters,
rocked by palms' rhythm and breeze
under blue, warm and cumulous,
I am rebirthed in another skin,
paint my toenails hibiscus pink,
wander barefoot the sandy streets,
paddle the waves with a Belizean dog;
undoing, mindless, loose as a fish.

My children in California, New York,
Pennsylvania,
are as far from their gimlet mother
as this village from the American way.
I think I'll stay. Detach. Go slack.
Contemplate the tide.
No one needs me but me.
What I need is ready to be found.

A papaya from the street market
has softened in the sun;
this morning it's ripe and
the blade sinks through.
A womb opens blood-red,
a goddess gleaming,
its hollow prodigal with seeds
dark and round, spilling
over like ovarian jewels.

I fill my mouth with such sweetness
as will sing through my veins forever.

II

There's a certain Slant of light....
—E. Dickinson

A CERTAIN KNOWLEDGE

Let me tell you what I know
about being shut out of heaven.
Let me tell you about a tiny boy,
18 months old.
His mother has a new baby.
His mother and baby brother are behind the closed door.

He hates what I have to offer:
milk and a teddy bear,
the rocking chair and a lullaby.
My heart twists with the red-cheeked howls,
the sweaty fists, the little feet planted.

Shut out of heaven cannot be cured.
Eventually, the new one will know,
as I, the old grandmother, know.
Such knowledge can never be undone
until death's compensation takes us in.

EVENING IN THE NURSING HOME

Suppertime in Skilled,
and folks are wheeled into the dining room,
bibbed and fed their vague purees—
The Bishop, the Doctor, the CEO,
the bald and faded Mother
hugging her smiling doll.

There is no rank here.
The aides do their jobs,
noting intake and calling it a day.
This one will not be here for breakfast.
That one will not remember how to swallow.

Outside the door the bold calendar
will soon be changed to say
TODAY is...
and another day, week, month and
year appear and disappear
right on time.

NANCY

Her Way

She was a natural leader,
knew her own moves, felt her own music.
But when Death approached,
she knew she would need to submit.
Still she insisted,
"I'll do this my way, thank you."

The dance began,
the slow waltz, unbearably lovely.
She led, her jaw set, her grasp firm.
Then the tempo quickened
and the struggle began.

Day after day she held her position
until ravaged and weary
she was ready to concede.
"Now, I'll follow," she whispered,
and was waltzed away.

Thirsty

As long as I knew her
she was thirsty as a desert,
she, whose garden grew lush and green,
who had everything she wanted
except justice for the poor, world peace,
respect and welcome for the scorned.
Still, the joke when we dined was
"Set the water by Nancy."

The view from her bed framed
a backyard stream, rippling in the sun.
As she weakened, she cried for water,
struggling to swallow the drops from a spoon
worse than useless for her desperate thirst.

How I longed to splash down her throat
great gulps of fresh water, her favorite drink.
How I longed to drench her
in living streams.

Hold Still

What thoughts, what words I clamp my teeth on.
Nancy, you are dying.
You can not care what to wear
and lie quietly in bed.
You can fold your restless hands
and close your searching eyes.

Nancy, hold still
so Death can catch you.

The Women Came

She asked, as the light failed,
if they could come to pray.
They came Tuesdays,
gathering around her chair
as around a cross,
kneeling or sitting on the floor,
close, touching her and each other.
Their petitions changed as the weeks went by—
Let it be beautiful.
Let it be kind.
Let it be soon.

Once when they were still able to sing,
they sang *Kyrie*, and she roused
suddenly
and joined in,
Lord, have mercy.

On the last day
their prayers came in sighs.
They kissed her and wandered home,
"It is finished," in their steps.
Rain was heavy in the cold
dark December.

The Burial

A small mercy, the blue sky
and sunshine, little clouds
bouncing in the wind.
No sound as the casket is lowered
except the grunt of the workmen doing their job.
But at the thud of the vault-lid
an anguished shudder breaks loose.

Even the ground clattering down is better,
especially
the tiny granddaughter caught up in the game
throwing handfuls in the grave,
a sister's fierce shoveling
and the falling roses.

When we sing a hymn
we hear the last word.
Not cancer, suffering, death;
not loneliness, sorrow, tears.
But hallelujah.
Hallelujah.

FIRST ANNIVERSARY

Let this past year's elements be gathered,
the bolt of anguish adhere to earthen ache,
and tears wet all.

A flawless July evening.
My little dog and I walk
the neighborhood, quiet;
she is watchful, fearful of big dogs.
We shun the street where they
rush out, clamoring.
But tonight, peaceful there, cool
in the shade. We move forward
confident
until a swift, silent stranger
streaks toward us and takes her.
Screams. Torn golden fur. Blood.
Death.
We are broken beyond words.
We are taken home.

Let the memory be held in my hands
solid and round like this blue bowl
from my sister's wheel.
She, too, lost painfully and too soon,
left her spirit in graced art.
Years later, she speaks to me
of beauty sweetening grief.

CONSIDER THE JAWS

My jaws are a dam
holding back a flood.
No wonder they hurt;
no wonder I can't chew,
laugh, sing, yawn…
My teeth knock together like rocks.

I consider other jaws:
Savage shark, killer whale
hungry with rage and terror,
Jaws of life
crunching a car to save the driver,
Jaw breakers,
the round dangerous treat of childhood.

I stood at an old man's grave
behind three stout sons.
They were motionless.
Their jaws throbbed like bagpipes.

DRAGON CAVE

Bellowing,
water boils out of rock,
steam rises in the blue air.
We stand at the door of a dragon
this sweet, safe day.

Science aside,
what is this rage, this menace,
this warning?
The brochure says we're long past due
for a volcanic eruption
that will blast this earth to rubble,
shred and melt the mountains,
blow us like debris into outer space.
Stay behind the fence,
reads an absurd sign to protect us
from the molten ocean
gaining force beneath us.

Is this the Apocalypse dragon,
red monster of seven heads and ten
horns? Its tail to thrash the universe,
a mouth belching
scalding water and flame?

Let's take a picture and be on our way.
Let's have a picnic at the park
a mile down the road.

AFRICAN VIOLETS

The table's thick with purple and pink,
luscious birds in furry nests
inhaling light, exhaling joy,

when a spore of powdery mildew
breathes on one, then another,
until all are pale and sick.
No sprays, treatments, methods,
wailing or prayer
can save them.

At last,
I carry them all to the fire
and give them over
to their own deaths.

I rub the table to a hard shine,
set down African Violets made in China.

MEASURING MY LIFE

On Tuesdays I swallow the pill for my bones
with a full glass of water, wait an hour
for breakfast, and stay upright.
Tuesdays march away. Here one comes again,
my life measured out week by week.

This morning the wild carrot thickens
the roadside with white lace.
A thousand locusts scream
that summer is ending as always.
The road mimics the seasons that control
what I wear, and the state of my mind.
It is Tuesday and August and morning
for these heartbeats, this mile.

I was young when I first walked here;
now I'm slower and more careful.
I pay out for my bones and heart, I pay out
my life like gold, Tuesday by Tuesday,
season by season, year by year…

OLD WOMEN

Everywhere I go these days I see old women—
A tiny one with mouse eyes
cradling a banana
exiting the dining room
of the retirement center.
A peevish one helping her teetering mate
edge his cane down the concrete steps
of the Glad Welcome Community Church.

Everywhere I go these days I watch
old women. Watch thin legs inch
along the sidewalk, making it home
with a bag of groceries and a clutched key.

Forgive my watching.
I cannot know how it will be for me,
but everywhere I go
these days I am trying to find out.

An old woman busy at the desk at the Y.
She has her body. She has her mind.
She has her means. I'll be her!
No doling out dollars at the drug counter,
hair in clumps, dress on backward
like a prescription for depression.
I'll keep everything needful until the Light strikes.
Please. Please?

STORIES

An old man told me
his parents visited my home
when he was four,
and he was allowed to touch the cheek
of my dead sister,
the baby I never saw,
that my parents never talked about.

A door opens
on a labyrinth
of images, questions,
astonished grief.

So much hidden, forgotten, gone,
numberless people
with countless stories,
each essential to the one.
Who can bear it?

And I too will take my stories
like dead babies
into the silence of the long sleep
where love knits an elastic border
and loses nothing.

III

PROVOCATIONS
*from The Gospel of Mark, TEV
The right time has come,
And the Kingdom of God is near!*
—Mark 1:14-15

In the beginning there was Time,
And Time moved like a child
In its crawling, toddling, running,
Until the Right Time
When a man on a hill,
Hourglass in hand,
Shouted news
Too edged to catch.

Centuries pass,
And still we miss,
And still,
Time and Kingdom come.

*

Whoever wants to be first must place himself last…
—Mark 9:33-37

Say that up is down,
Declare that rich is poor,
Argue that gain is loss,
And I will ask
If last is first.

Preach that grief is joy,
Insist that fools are wise,
Prove that death is life,
And I will believe
That last is first.

*

Don't take anything with you on the trip...
—Mark 6:7-13

Go out empty, spare
And simple.
Don't pack comfort
Or even need.
Let your empty hand heal,
Your plain word bless.
Go spare,
(Except for the burden
Balanced light
Across your shoulders.)

*

Who is my Mother?
—Mark 3:31-35

How could you say it
To your own mother,
Your trusting brothers,
"You are no more to me than anyone
Who obeys God?"

Does blood mean nothing?
Is name a passing sound?
Is spirit as real as flesh?
Does faith bear family?
Is God first?

*

No one shall ever eat figs from you again!
—Mark 11:12-14, 20-24

Seems unlearned
To seek a fig
When figs are not in season.

Seems unjust
To curse a tree
That only needed time.

Seems unsound
To use a pique
To teach disciples lessons.

Seems unwise
To move a hill
To make a poem rhyme.

Lord,
Are things not always
As they seem?

*

You are no more intelligent than the others...
—Mark 7:14-23

You have been sought, taught,
Explained to, cradled,
Coddled.
You have known my most intimate
Moments, shared my deepest thoughts,
Heard my plainest words,
And still you don't hear,
Don't see, don't understand –
Witless ones!
You are as stupid
As the rest!

*

It isn't right to take the children's food and throw it to the dogs.
—Mark 7:25-30

Wish I'd have seen your eyes,
Jesus, when you said that—
Must have been a twinkle there,
A sly quirk at your lips, enjoying
Your jest with a quick-witted woman
Who wasn't shy at asking,
Knew she was as good as any Jew,
And didn't cry at being called
A dog.
Thanks, Lord, for the pinch of pepper;
Thanks for teasing and healing us foreigners.

*

What do you want me to do for you?
—Mark 10:46-52

Dirty, mangy, noisy, ridiculous
Beggar.
Blind, but so what,
Sure deserves what he got,
And the brass to bawl
Like an old goat
Disrupting our discussion
With the master.
Just who does he think he is?

And the King of kings,
Lord of lords,
Stops to inquire:
What do you want me to do for you?

You'd think he was a servant.

*

Whoever is not against us is for us.
—Mark 9:38-41

But Lord—
They chant,
They wear crucifixes,
They buy bumper stickers,

They feast,
They fast,
They beat drums,
They withhold taxes,
They join the army,
They pray in tongues,
They live in monasteries,
They preach in the streets—

All together now,
Jesus is Lord!

*

This Man
—Mark 5:1-20

It's not that I run
Naked and howling
Through graveyards,
Bruising and gashing myself
On stones.

It's just that I
Waver on the edge
Of an abyss of
Fear
Ravenous
To possess
My mind.

And I want more than I can say
The sweet health of this good man
And to be near him always.

*

Father! My Father!
—Mark 14:32-36. 15:34

Without glands, God could not weep.
Without muscle, God could not wring his hands.
Without bone, God could not pace the floor.
Without flesh, God could not get wretchedly sick.

What then
Did God do
To endure
The agony
Of a
Son?

*

Who will roll away the stone?
—Mark 16:1-4

Watch out for a dazzling omen,
That surprises you in strange places,
Moving stones from the mouth of miracles

To set you running like a spooked
Hallelujah.

It could be an Easter morning.

IV

I dwell in Possibility
—E. Dickinson

ALL SUMMER BLUE

All summer a bluebird knocked at my window,
stared at me with surprised and baleful eyes,
said, "What're you looking at?"
and flew off in a spit of blue.

All summer I watched the morning glories open,
pressed my face against theirs,
breathed their new cool,
crawled in and slept on their blue silk.

One thick afternoon in August,
a breeze blew away the haze.
I looked up and saw an angel
spinning swirls of blue
beyond blue.

CAROLINA BANKS

You have sand like cream
and tides that rush your senses,
breezes teasing your skin
and a melted sun,
sky turned over like a blue bowl
with clouds of cotton kisses.

People come here to be healed.
They loll and play,
glean shells, ride waves and stroll.
They sit for hours with half-closed eyes
to forget and to remember.

What they forget drowses on the ocean floor, dreaming.
What they remember leaps like dolphins cresting the horizon.

DREAMS

She woke to the heaviness of bad dreams.
Before she could stop them, one voice after another
announced their findings: her sins, sorrows, stupidities,
humiliations, mistakes, misfortunes: A lifetime of trash.
She got up and piled it on the bed,
gathered the four corners of the sheet,
tied them together into a bundle,
threw it across her shoulder and flew out the window.

The landfill was too crowded with trash trucks,
the ocean and forest too beautiful to despoil.
A cave and a canyon didn't want her either.
Rain and wind washed over her. The sun
warmed her as she flew in and out of clouds.
She felt her burden lighten, and turning to look,
saw that the sheet was empty. She flew home,
tucked it smooth on the bed, lay down,
and fell asleep to peaceful dreams.

INSOMNIA

I am sitting in the living room
at 3:00 A.M.
eating graham crackers
in the dark

because insomnia is hard work,
and even though I think of
people lying awake in anguish
losing loved ones, health, job or home,
(terrible things coming to me too
but not tonight as far as I know)
and even though I think of
poems about insomnia
written by excellent poets,
still, I'm weary and hungry
and a little depressed.
I remember myself, a Mennonite farm child
and dreamless ten hour nights in a snug bed
having graham crackers and milk for supper
Sunday evenings before all the family went
to church, comfort food of a homiest kind.
So I am really okay
sitting here in the dark
with crumbs coming down
on my nightgown
and into the carpet
where in the morning
the dog will sniff and search.

HEAVEN

Small boys at play talk about heaven.
One doesn't want to go,
golden streets or not,
not even if it's true that
You can ride a rhinoceros in heaven.

At bedtime I let the dog out
and while she searches the yard
I look up through branches of birch
that frame a half-moon and a star.

Some strange evidence seizes me
as though I stand in a direct line
from my patch of grass right up
through the tree, through the night sky,
and on to the moon,
and on to the star and on to
something beyond, maybe even
a rhinoceros snuffling a golden street,
a five-year-old grinning on its back.

VILLANELLE

You don't have to live any life but your own,
the grief of the world is grief that will stay.
Keep feeding the river, the river goes on.

Gray seeps through my eyelids closed to the dawn
that spews out commuters into the fray.
You don't have to live any life but your own.

The blankets are soft against my old bones.
No nights with sick children, needing to pray.
Keep feeding the river, the river goes on.

I watch at the sidelines; the stars that once shone
are dropping the ball as they work the replay.
You don't have to live any life but your own.

Years of the quest for achievement are gone.
Did something I started bring good that will stay?
Keep feeding the river, the river goes on.

Life beckons and leads to the great white way
where souls add their spark at the end of the day.
You don't have to live any life but your own.
Keep feeding the river, the river goes on.

THE WORD

We wander in the deep woods
as night is falling.
The white winter sun, so dear
and distant, has sunk
to the bone chill of last light.
Black branches lower their
swarthy arms.
Are we now truly lost
to know only the dark night?

In a pocket you find a stub of candle
and one match. A flicker speaks a word
against the dark. The word names
the next step. My tight heart calms
as we inch along.
The calm holds no conclusion;
who knows how the black woods spread?
But a word as small as a spark
keeps us on a path that leads forward.

HANGING ON

Decrepit but indomitable
they totter from walker to chair
in a clutter of medicine and
equipment for keeping alive.
I carry the scene home
and sleepless at 3:00 a.m.
get a drink and sit up in bed
listening to the mockingbird.

Loud and clear, his notes dazzle,
splashing me
in a lyric fountain.
People kill them for just such singing.

I'm 70. I can sit up in bed all night,
drinking tea and listening,
thinking about indomitable
decrepitude. I can be
what I am. I can live like
a mockingbird and die
hanging on to every note I've got.

EASTER VISIT

The state hospital meets old expectations:
Gates, walls, locks,
dark halls, bareness and chill.
I come again and again all winter
but my words, hands, prayers, and presence
fail in grace. I go home,
wishing her rest even in death.

Today it's April. I go without words
bearing lilacs in a paper cup.
Her stark face bows into the fragrance.
She does not speak or look up
but turns back to her ward,
moving like a soul at prayer,
breathing a rising purple radiance.

THE BOWL

The young minister, how winsome he is,
surrounded by children who fidget and shove,
telling them a story. My grandsons lean into
the circle while my heart leans into love.

He holds up broken pieces of a bowl.
The children move closer, helping in turn
to glue it together. I watch how it fits;
the cracks form a jagged pattern.

The congregation smiles, not knowing that
soon, very soon, he will resign,
disgraced by drunkenness and sex,
get out of sight with his broken design.

Years later, I think about him still,
the poetry of his words and mood,
the memory of his jagged truth,
the way our broken vessels can be glued.

AFTER THE EVENING NEWS

After the bombardment
of broken and bleeding terror,
after the rage of the weather
exploding on the wailing earth,
after the planned and random violence
that daily assaults the planet,
I carry the News to the garden.

Swallowtails in swirls sip zinnias,
inviting me among them.
They float against my shoulders,
tiptoe, tasting the sweetness;
undulating wings are waves
of yellow, blue, and black.

From a cocoon of darkness
they raise their wings to the sun
for this day, on this planet.

MOVING THE BEES

The hive was half hidden by weeds
as bees charted their course all summer.
Through fields of blossoms they labored,
a union of workers behind their queen
and the loyals who fed her.

The beekeeper's deep polished voice
could break over lost bees.
He taped the hive closed
one damp, chilled evening
when some were still in the field.
They returned, shut out and confused,
circling, trying all night to get in.
Morning dawned and the beekeeper
loaded the hive for another field
and drove away.

The shut-out ones refused to be lost.
They beat their tiny wings
and followed their queen.

THE FIELD

Field seems hardly the word for it,
imaging up green crops, a golden harvest;
here instead a tangle of weeds and rocks,
broken down fence and scrub cedar,
the sponge of a hidden spring.
At least, crossing it, I'm not hardening
light soil or trampling corn. Whoever
owns it will not mind my passing through.

My passing through becomes a rite—
Feet will go this way, wearing a path.
My eyes see more, ears hear, all senses
opening to the life throbbing in this place.
Little gifts come into my hands,
my conscience free as I pick milkweed
and wild carrot, carry home a smooth stone,
even cut a tiny cedar for Christmas.

The field is becoming mine, the rabbits
and birds, companions. As the seasons
come and go, my belonging deepens
until a spring when the truth dawns
like Easter. My life is here.
I must find the owner and pay.
I will cash in all of my scattered assets
to buy this field where my treasure lies.

WALK IN NOVEMBER

Be comforted by austere November air.
Be comforted by the sound of moving water.
Be comforted by the honest absence of birds.
Be comforted by the gray plumes of squirrels.

Be roused by bronze certainties of leaves.
Be teased by the smell of sleeping woods.
Be nudged by stones worn smooth.
Be reborn by memories of the dead.

November, who is your comforter?
Earth, who is your mother?

WATCHING CANDLES ON CHRISTMAS EVE

Seven identical souls, Christ-child white,
line up along the candelabra
awaiting their entrance as heralding stars.
On Christmas Eve I light them;
five perform clean and sedate,
an Episcopal choir,
while two run ravenous, eating down
their throats, rivulets dribbling
to crazed shapes.

Is this a destiny of draft or flawed tallow?
A tainted station, second instead of first,
fourth instead of sixth?
I spread newspaper and watch them go,
swallowing themselves, piling waste
and blinking out.

Five trim souls go on praising,
raising their eyes,
scrupulous as saints.

AT CENTERING PRAYER

I hear breathing
somewhere out there
in the vast sanctuary
of Holy Spirit Episcopal.

Our little group is silent,
motionless. We listen.
What I hear
is someone humming,
someone who knows
the system
and keeps it running.

Somewhere out there
the Custodian
hums and breathes and
soaks up our prayer.

We bow to each other and
steal away. . . .

TO THE MOUNTAIN

Like a god risen
with the sun at her back,
Squaw Peak in the morning.
Essential. Lifted up
from earth, a mother
of brown rock, crevassed twig,
bloomy spine.

Thank you for doing nothing
but
being there
for small, scurrying ones
to crawl on and question.

"Love your life," you reply.
"Love every tedious beat
of your dear and fleeting life."

LONGING FOR FREEDOM

I woke this morning
from obsessed dreams
longing for freedom.

I was yelling at my friend,
hating the way she didn't hear,
wanting to free the tears sealed
in the closet of my throat.
I feared her shrugged shoulder.
Whose turn is it to get
what we want or need?
How do we escape
tangled attachment?

Maybe dying, I think as I peel
a banana and pour the milk.
Maybe death is the sill to a freedom
so pure we are lifted into a light and
fragrant air, into color inconceivable,
into a new realm of joyful abandon
beyond boundary, let loose together.

I carry my breakfast to the porch
to watch the morning glories open.
Every day they astound my eyes
as I gaze into their perfect blue faces.
This morning a vine has leaped beyond
the top of the trellis and is wandering
back and forth in the empty air
with no place to cling.

THERE IS A WAY

There is a way—
There is always a way.

It may take ten lifetimes.
It may use up a sea of tears,
Years spent sitting in the dark.

But the bent wisp of grass
Will whisper direction,
A word in the world's thesaurus
Will rise from a page,
A fine, sharp blade
Will find the space between joints.

There is a way—
There is always a way,

Sifting, sifting with an aching back
Till the glint of gold takes the eye;
The nudging at a door for
A crack and a ray and the scent of air.

There is a way,
There is always a way,
Even the sweep of the mortician's flame,
And the light bright gust upward.

THE AUTHOR

Barbara Esch's first poems were written on her family's farm in Pigeon, Michigan where she was born and grew up with five brothers and sisters. After high school, (Eastern Mennonite, Harrisonburg, Virginia) she married Harold Shisler and made a home with him and their three children in eastern Pennsylvania. A job in a group home for intellectually disabled adults grew into a call to pastoral ministry at Indian Creek Foundation, a Mennonite-affiliated agency. Leadership roles in her Perkasie Mennonite congregation led to a place on the pastoral team and ordination by Franconia Mennonite Conference.

Since retirement, she has continued her involvement at Perkasie Mennonite in various roles, including coordinating mental health ministry and leading the Faith and Light chapter of the international organization of communities started by Jean Vanier in France.

She and Harold have been married nearly sixty years. Their family has grown from three children to include three spouses, four grandchildren, and a grandson-in-law. Writing has been a lifelong joy and learning with publications in books and periodicals. At home in a small house in an adult community, she cherishes family and friends, walks with her dog, gardening, books, movies, and much more.

www.ingramcontent.com/pod-product-compliance
Lightning Source LLC
Chambersburg PA
CBHW051349040426
42453CB00007B/485